Office for Disarmament Affairs

Verification in all its aspects, including the role of the United Nations in the field of verification

United Nations

New York, 2008

GUIDE TO THE USER

This print publication, available in all official languages, has been issued in implementation of the United Nations Disarmament Information Programme as a handy, convenient and attractive reference tool containing the report of the Secretary-General on verification in all its aspects, including the role of the United Nations in the field of verification.

In a modest departure from previously released Study Series, this publication contains not only the report of the Secretary-General, but additional material related to the publication of the report.

The publication continues the Disarmament Study Series (a full list of titles of the "Blue Book" series is available on page iii) and should serve as a valuable addition to the reference section of public and university libraries, permanent missions, research institutes and specialized non-governmental organizations.

For the electronic version of all material contained in this Study Series, see http://disarmament.un.org/DDApublications/index.html.

Symbols of United Nations documents are composed of capital letters combined with figures. Mention of such a symbol indicates a reference to a United Nations document.

UNITED NATIONS PUBLICATION
Sales No. E.08.IX.5
ISBN 978-92-1-142262-7

Copyright © United Nations, 2008
All rights reserved

List of "Blue Book" *Study Series*

No.	Year	Title
32	2008	Verification in all its aspects, including the role of the United Nations in the field of verification
31	2005	The relationship between disarmament and development in the current international context
30	2003	Study on disarmament and non-proliferation education
29	2003	The issue of missiles in all its aspects
28	1999	Small Arms
27	1994	Study on the Application of Confidence-building Measures in Outer Space
26	1993	Study on Defensive Security Concepts and Policies
25	1993	Potential Uses of Military-Related Resources for Protection of the Environment
24	1992	Study on Ways and Means of Promoting Transparency in International Transfers of Conventional Arms
23	1991	South Africa's Nuclear-Tipped Ballistic Missile Capability
22	1991	Effective and Verifiable Measures Which Would Facilitate the Establishment of a Nuclear-weapon-free Zone in the Middle East
21	1991	Nuclear Weapons: A Comprehensive Study
20	1991	The role of the United Nations in the Field of Verification
19	1989	Study on the Economic and Social Consequences of the Arms Race and Military Expenditures
18	1989	Study on the Climatic and Other Global Effects of Nuclear War
17	1987	Study on Deterrence
16	1986	The Naval Arms Race
15	1986	Reduction of Military Budgets
14	1986	Concepts of Security
13	1985	Unilateral Nuclear Disarmament Measures
12	1985	Study on Conventional Disarmament
11	1983	Economic and Social Consequences of the Arms Race and of Military Expenditures
10	1983	Reduction of Military Budgets
9	1983	The Implications of Establishing an International Satellite Monitoring Agency
8	1982	Relationship between Disarmament and International Security
7	1982	Comprehensive Study on Confidence-building Measures
6	1982	Study on Israeli Nuclear Armament
5	1982	The Relationship between Disarmament and Development (see also No. 31, 2005)
4	1981	Reduction of Military Budgets
3	1981	Study on all the aspects of Regional Disarmament
2	1981	South Africa's plan and capability in the nuclear field
1	1981	Comprehensive Study on Nuclear Weapons (see also No. 21, 1991)

Printed copies may be obtained by consulting your local bookstore or through the United Nations Publications website: https://unp.un.org.

Verifying Non-Proliferation and Disarmament Agreements Today

DDA Occasional Paper No. 10, March 2006

This paper was prepared in order to more widely disseminate the presentations made at the panel discussion held on 20 October 2005, organized by the Department for Disarmament Affairs (DDA) and the Government of Canada, which has taken a leading role in the promotion of multilateral verification of disarmament and non-proliferation agreements for many years.

For the electronic version, please visit our website at http://disarmament.un.org/DDApublications/op10.htm.

Contents

Paragraphs *Page*

Part 1 **A/61/1028**
Report of the Panel of Government Experts on verification in all its aspects, including the role of the United Nations in the field of verification 1

    Foreword by the Secretary-General 2

    Letter of transmittal... 3

    List of presentations made by verification analysts and practitioners from the United Nations, its Member States and its family of organizations, from non-governmental research institutions and associations..................................... 7

  I. Introduction 1–8   9

 II. Purpose of verification.................................... 9–28   11

III. Evolution of the concept of verification since 1995 29–40   14

IV. Verification methods, procedures and technologies 41–57   17

 V. Verification and compliance mechanisms 58–71   20

VI. Final recommendation 72   22

Part 2 **Background material**... 23

  I. General Assembly resolutions and note 23

    A. A/RES/62/21 (which commends the report to the attention of Member States)... 23

    B. Note of the General Assembly of 8 December 2005 24

    C. A/RES/59/60 (which called for views of Member States and set up the Panel of Experts) 24

 II. Sixteen Principles of Verification 25

III. Views of Member States (excerpted from A/60/96 and Add.1 and 2) 27

Part 1

A/61/1028
Report of the Panel of Government Experts on verification in all its aspects, including the role of the United Nations in the field of verification

Summary

The international security environment has changed considerably over the past decade, with corresponding implications for non-proliferation, arms control, disarmament and confidence-building measures. These changes have also had implications for verification in general and led to a greater emphasis on compliance with obligations under existing treaties, agreements and commitments. They have also fostered a greater realization of the need to respond to non-compliance with arrangements in force and to build national capacities to implement them more fully and effectively.

Pursuant to the request made by the General Assembly in its resolution 59/60, the Secretary-General established a panel of government experts to prepare a study on verification in all its aspects, including the role of the United Nations in the field of verification. Two previous United Nations expert reports on the subject, in 1990 and 1995, dealt comprehensively with the issue. Building on those reports, the current Panel approaches the issue selectively, looking at what has changed in 10 years and discerning new trends and developments.

The experts examine the purpose of verification; its conceptual evolution; developing methods, procedures and technologies; and verification and compliance mechanisms. The Panel offers 21 generic recommendations for active consideration by Member States, treaty bodies or the United Nations.

Foreword by the Secretary-General

Verification of compliance went hand in glove during the 1990s, with the remarkable gains made in multilateral disarmament and arms control. A new era of global cooperation in ensuring the effective implementation of treaties seemed to be dawning — the Chemical Weapons Convention set out the most far-reaching verification arrangements ever made with regard to a disarmament agreement, and the establishment of the Preparatory Commission for the Comprehensive Nuclear-Test-Ban Treaty initiated the development of a worldwide network of monitoring stations and a global communications system that was unprecedented in scope. Two comprehensive United Nations government expert reports on verification in 1990 and 1995 underscored this trend. Verification was accepted as a tool to reinforce disarmament agreements, thus enhancing national and international peace and security.

However, the tide turned in the first years of this century, and the famous catch-phrase of the cold war, "trust and verify", became tarnished. It is thus encouraging to see that the present report, the third in the series, acknowledges a shift away from that perception. The report upholds the need for verification of arms agreements, treaties and other commitments and highlights the responsibility of States to comply with those commitments. It also recognizes how rapidly technical advances are being applied to verification and compliance commitments. It stresses that new areas of international cooperation, such as controls on the illicit trade in small arms and lights weapons, call for fresh thinking about monitoring of compliance at the regional and subregional levels.

The experts do not propose specific solutions for the verification of international arms norms, but they do suggest that solutions can be found. Those solutions could generate greater levels of confidence among States. I share the hope expressed in the final recommendation made by the Panel that Member States will consider actively how to further develop the 21 recommendations made by the Panel. The focus of the purpose remains *trust* among States. That trust can be built and strengthened through effective verification, compliance and monitoring.

Letter of transmittal

[30 July 2007]

I have the honour to submit herewith the report of the Panel of Government Experts on verification in all its aspects, including the role of the United Nations in the field of verification. The Panel was appointed in pursuance of paragraph 3 of General Assembly resolution 59/60 of 3 December 2004. The experts appointed to the Panel are listed at the end of the present letter.

As Chairman of the Panel, I am pleased to inform you that consensus was reached on the report. Arriving at consensus was achieved through a combination of face-to-face meetings, electronic communications and telephonic exchanges — an approach that afforded additional time and opportunity to pursue consultations and discussions. These latter permitted the Panel to iron out last divergences on the text.

The Panel's work

The Panel held three sessions last year: 30 January-3 February 2006 in New York; 8-12 May 2006 in Geneva; and 7-11 August 2006 in New York.

The Panel's deliberations were enriched by presentations made by several of its members in their respective areas of verification and compliance expertise. Throughout the sessions, the Panel also heard presentations by verification analysts and practitioners from within the United Nations, its Member States and its family of organizations, as well as from non-governmental research institutes and associations. The Panel wishes to express its gratitude to these experts for their contributions. A list of the presentations is annexed to the present letter.

On the last day of its third session, the Panel found that more time was needed to continue work on the draft text. Much solid work had been achieved and it was agreed that the end of the formal face-to-face meetings should not spell the conclusion of all efforts to reach a consensus text. Consequently, the Panel entrusted the Chairman with the task of continuing consultations through electronic means to resolve the outstanding differences on the text during the time before a report would formally have to be submitted.

On 16 October 2006, upon the request of the Chairperson of the First Committee of the General Assembly, I gave an interim report on the work of the Panel to the Committee. In it, I explained to members of the First Committee that, though the time allotted for formal sessions had expired, the Panel was still resolved to continue working towards a consensus report, particularly given the important contribution such a consensus could make to establishing a common view on the role of verification with respect to disarmament and arms control agreements.

On 6 December 2006, the General Assembly, by decision 61/514, encouraged the Panel to bring its work to an agreed conclusion as soon as possible, and decided to include the item on the agenda of the next session of the Assembly. On 27 June 2007, the Panel reached agreement on the text which is attached to this letter of transmittal. I would point out that the substantive work of the Panel was conducted during 2006. The content of the report therefore reflects issues relating to verification as of August 2006.

Throughout the Panel's deliberations in 2006 — during the formal meetings as well as the subsequent procedure of electronic consultations — the members of the Panel were strongly supported by the Under-Secretary-General for Disarmament Affairs. The Panel members are grateful for his repeated reminders to the Panel of the timeliness of its work and his continuing encouragement to reach an agreed conclusion.

The Panel wishes also to express appreciation for the invaluable contribution of three verification experts, from both within and outside the United Nations system, who served as consultants to the Panel: the Director of the United Nations Institute for Disarmament Research; the Deputy Director of the Verification Research, Training and Information Centre; and the Director of the Canadian Centre for Treaty Compliance at Carleton University in Ottawa. The Panel also wishes to express appreciation to the Chief of the Monitoring, Database and Information Branch of the Office for Disarmament Affairs, who served as Secretary of the Group, and to other Secretariat officials who assisted the Panel with their expertise.

(*Signed*) John **Barrett**
Chairman of the Panel

The government experts appointed to the Panel were the following:

Masahiko Asada
Professor of International Law
Kyoto University Graduate School of Law
Kyoto, Japan

John Barrett
Director-General
Strategic Planning Bureau
Department of Foreign Affairs and International Trade of Canada
Ottawa

Volodymyr Belashov
Director
Directorate General for Arms Control and Military-Technical Cooperation
Ministry of Foreign Affairs of Ukraine
Kiev

Michael Biontino
Head of the Conventional Arms Control and Verification Unit
Ministry of Foreign Affairs of Germany
Berlin

Choi Hong-ghi
Counsellor
Permanent Mission of the Republic of Korea to the United Nations
New York

Machiel Combrink
Deputy Director, Nuclear and Non-Proliferation
Department of Foreign Affairs of South Africa
Pretoria

Philippe Errera
Deputy Director, Centre for Analysis and Policy Planning
Ministry of Foreign Affairs of France
Paris

Sally K. Horn
Senior Adviser to the Assistant Secretary
Bureau of Verification, Compliance and Implementation
United States Department of State
Washington, D.C.

Samantha Job
First Secretary
Permanent Mission of the United Kingdom of Great Britain
 and Northern Ireland to the United Nations
New York

Pablo Macedo
Deputy Permanent Representative of Mexico to the United Nations
 Office in Geneva
Geneva

R. Carlos Sersale di Cerisano
Ambassador of Argentina to South Africa
Pretoria

Björn Skala
Ambassador
Ministry for Foreign Affairs of Sweden
Stockholm

Chuka Udedibia
Minister
Permanent Mission of Nigeria to the United Nations
New York

Victor L. Vasiliev
Deputy Director, Department of International Organizations
Ministry of Foreign Affairs of the Russian Federation
Moscow

Aruni Wijewardane
Permanent Representative of Sri Lanka to the United Nations
 Office at Vienna
Vienna

Zhang Yan
Director-General, Department of Arms Control and Disarmament
Ministry of Foreign Affairs of China
Beijing

List of presentations made by verification analysts and practitioners from the United Nations, its Member States and its family of organizations, from non-governmental research institutions and associations

Beck, Volker. Coordinator of the 1540 (2004) experts. *Security Council resolution 1540 (2004).*

Bosch, Olivia. Senior Research Fellow, International Security Programme at Chatham House (Royal Institute of International Affairs), London. *Issues of non-proliferation of weapons of mass destruction, in particular on Security Council resolution 1540 (2004).*

Buchanan, Ewen. Public Information Officer, United Nations Monitoring, Verification and Inspection Commission. *United Nations verification: Iraq weapons of mass destruction.*

Buisson, Mike. Member of the Group of Experts monitoring the implementation of Security Council resolution 1654 (2006). *Sanctions and arms embargo.*

Carle, Christophe. Deputy Director, United Nations Institute for Disarmament Research, United Nations Office at Geneva. *Missiles.*

Cassandra, Michael. Chief, Monitoring, Database and Information Branch, Department for Disarmament Affairs. *The work of the Department for Disarmament Affairs in the area of verification.*

DeSutter, Paula A. United States Assistant Secretary of State for Verification, Compliance and Implementation. *The Libya model: strategic commitment and verification.*

Ghita-Duminica, Adrian. Senior Adviser, Industry, Canadian National Authority. *Verification through routine on-site inspections at industrial facilities under the Chemical Weapons Convention: views of a former inspector.*

Gizowski, Sylwin. Strategic Coordination and Planning Officer, Office of the Executive Secretary, Preparatory Commission of the Comprehensive Nuclear-Test-Ban Treaty Organization. *International monitoring system.*

Goldschmidt, Pierre. Member of the Board of Directors and of the Executive Committee of the Association Vinçotte Nucléaire, Visiting Scholar with Carnegie Endowment for International Peace and former Deputy Director General, Head of the Department of Safeguards, International Atomic Energy Agency. *Nuclear issues.*

Krepon, Michael. Co-founder of the Henry L. Stimson Center, Washington, D.C. *Cooperative threat reduction.*

McDonald, Glenn. Yearbook Coordinator, Senior Researcher, Small Arms Survey. *Verification, including monitoring, reporting, inspection and confidence-building aspects which apply to small arms agreements.*

Reeps, Horst. Director of Verification, Organization for the Prohibition of Chemical Weapons. *The verification process.*

Smithson, Amy. Senior Fellow at Centre for Strategic and International Studies, Washington, D.C. *Issues related to chemical and biological weapons proliferation.*

Stoffer, Howard. Head of Administration and Information, Counter-Terrorism Committee Executive Directorate. *Developments in methods, procedures and technologies for verification of compliance in the light of international experiences.*

Wareham, Mary. International Committee to Ban Landmines, former Coordinator of Landmine Monitor. *Development of verification and compliance with the Mine Ban Convention.*

Yehl, Tom. Director of Technology and Assessment, Bureau of Verification, Compliance and Implementation, United States Department of State. *Cooperative methodologies and technologies for verification and compliance assessment.*

Zanders, Jean Pascal. Bio Weapons Prevention Project. *Verification in support of the prevention of the weaponization of disease: challenges and options.*

Zlauvinen, Gustavo. Representative of the Director General of the International Atomic Energy Agency to the United Nations and Director of the New York Office. *Developments at the International Atomic Energy Agency with respect to verification.*

I. Introduction

1. In the 11 years since the last United Nations expert group report on verification (A/50/377), the international security environment has changed considerably, with corresponding implications for non-proliferation, arms control, disarmament and confidence-building measures. Global terrorism has made its baneful impact felt in many States, reinforcing concern about the potential for terrorists to obtain and use chemical, biological, radiological or nuclear weapons. An international clandestine network for the procurement of designs, materials and technologies for nuclear weapons has been discovered. Non-compliance with obligations arising from the Treaty on the Non-Proliferation of Nuclear Weapons and nuclear safeguards agreements has occurred, with one State announcing its withdrawal from the Treaty. Advances in biotechnology and genetics have emerged that have profound implications for the control of biological and toxin weapons. Missile proliferation is also of concern in this context as more States have acquired knowledge and capacity to develop, produce and deploy means of delivery, including missiles, and other unmanned systems that can be used in a destabilizing manner. There is also a growing risk of misuse of dual-use technologies and items.

2. In the area of conventional arms, armed conflicts in various regions have been exacerbated by the illicit transfer from outside sources of certain types of weapons, particularly small arms and light weapons, including weapons of increasing sophistication and destructiveness.

3. Such changes in the international security environment have implications for non-proliferation, arms control and disarmament as well as for confidence-building and verification. In addition, there is growing emphasis on full compliance by all States with their obligations under existing treaties, agreements and commitments, as well as growing realization of the importance of responding to non-compliance[1] and building national capacities to implement those treaties, agreements and commitments more fully and effectively. This has stimulated renewed discussion on the purpose, effectiveness and relevance of verification in its capacity to promote compliance and to deter, detect and help to address non-compliance.

4. Over the past decade, the technical means of verification have continued to evolve, providing a greater range of tools that can be used, including those within the grasp of a wider number of States and organizations. The rapid advancement of information and communications technology, including most notably the Internet, has broadened considerably the availability of relevant information and placed such information within the grasp not only of States and international organizations but also of civil society. It has also led to challenges related to the sheer amount and variable quality of information available. But, in parallel, it has produced major

---

[1] Unless otherwise indicated, in the context of the present report, the term non-compliance is used in a general sense and not as it is used in any specific treaty.

improvements in data gathering, processing, search and retrieval capabilities that have facilitated the identification of information relevant to verification.

5. Advances in remote sensing, including by satellite and aerial means, and their growing commercial availability at reasonable cost, have expanded access to information relevant to verification. Improved sampling and analysing techniques have furthermore increased the capacity of States to gather relevant information for verification purposes.

6. The experience and accumulated expertise of international agencies, standing verification bodies and bilateral and regional arrangements for verification and monitoring have provided a valuable contribution and have enriched and helped to spur the development of new approaches, methods and technologies for verification. An ever-expanding number of personnel is gaining experience in verification, including as on-site inspectors in various fields, thereby giving more and more States a role in the conduct of verification.

7. Verification also has its constraints. Questions have been raised about the efficacy of verification approaches, technologies and methodologies for detecting non-compliance with certain types of obligations in a timely manner. Recent experience has shown that, in respect of some types of activities, including procurement and development of dual-use items and certain types of weapons, efforts to violate obligations may not be detectable or confirmable as illicit. An appropriate balance must be found between the needs of verification, on the one hand, and legitimate national security and commercial proprietary concerns, on the other hand. The capacity of States to implement their obligations can be inadequate. For example, some States have serious problems in monitoring and implementing legal controls on the activities of individuals and non-governmental entities within their territory.

8. Keeping in mind both the need to avoid duplication of work done by the earlier panels (see A/45/372 and Corr.1 and A/50/379) and General Assembly guidelines on report writing, this report is selective, not exhaustive, in its treatment of verification. Within these parameters, the Panel has sought to focus in particular on what has changed in the decade since the last report and what is different in the international community's approach to, and understanding of, verification, in order to discern new trends and requirements. It includes established verification approaches as well as emerging approaches that support verification. To this end, the Panel has examined the purpose of verification; the evolution of the concept of verification since 1995; verification methods, procedures and technologies; and, verification and compliance mechanisms. Examination of the verification "toolbox" has been undertaken with a view to suggesting areas in which additional work could usefully be pursued. In addition, the Panel has looked at the key factors influencing what States want and expect from verification and how these expectations might be addressed. The overall objective was to produce a report with forward-looking recommendations, which States are invited to explore and examine and to take up in their own right.

II. Purpose of verification

9. Verification is a tool to strengthen international security. It involves the collection, collation and analysis of information in order to make a judgement as to whether a party is complying with its obligations. Such obligations may derive from treaties, agreements or arrangements or from decisions of competent multilateral organs such as the Security Council.

10. Most non-proliferation, arms control and disarmament regimes have been conceived to include formal, legally binding bilateral or multilateral verification arrangements. Such arrangements set out the procedures, methodologies and technologies for the conduct of verification and for addressing concerns related to parties' activities. More recently, some States also have utilized less formal arrangements.

11. States may develop cooperative verification arrangements either informally or through the establishment of bilateral, multilateral (including regional) or international bodies. In addition, or alternatively, they may use their own national means and methods of verification. Cooperative verification mechanisms can be useful to all States, particularly to those with limited national capacity and resources for conducting their own verification and monitoring activities. Although some forms of participation in verification may be costly, States derive significant security and other benefits from treaty membership.

12. There is no single means of verification applicable to all agreements. Parties to each arrangement, treaty or agreement will select from a range of verification tools the means that they deem necessary, effective and acceptable. Factors that affect the design of verification arrangements include the nature of the obligations and activities to be verified; national security concerns; the risks associated with and the potential impact of non-compliance; the compliance history of the parties involved; the degree of trust between the parties; commercial confidentiality; the benefits and costs of the contemplated means of verification; the availability of alternative or additional resources, including national means and methods of verification; the need to avoid misuse or abuse of verification; and the principles of reciprocity and impartiality. Each State may give different weight to these factors.

13. Multilateral, treaty-bound verification is a desirable goal. It can enhance credibility, encourage universality, bring all participating States together in a common endeavour, help to build transparency and confidence and facilitate compliance. It can also facilitate action, where applicable, by implementation bodies, the General Assembly and the Security Council to bring States parties back into compliance. However, there is a concern that such arrangements may not always be appropriate or feasible.

14. The political will of States to implement non-proliferation, arms control and disarmament obligations and commitments, including confidence-building measures, and to participate in the associated verification arrangements, where

applicable, is crucial. It is characterized by the willingness of States to share information, allocate resources, use available verification mechanisms and deal with cases of non-compliance. If provided with sufficient flexibility and sturdiness, the verification arrangements will be better able to meet and withstand crises should they arise.

15. Various international organizations play a role in multilateral monitoring and verification. For example, the International Atomic Energy Agency (IAEA) and the Organization for the Prohibition of Chemical Weapons (OPCW) contribute to increasing effective verification, including by promoting training activities, optimizing the utilization of monitoring and verification resources, maintaining extensive and accessible databases in their respective fields and providing technical and other assistance to participating States to comply fully with their obligations. Additionally, while the Comprehensive Nuclear-Test-Ban Treaty is not in force, work is under way in the Preparatory Commission for the Comprehensive Nuclear-Test-Ban Treaty Organization to build an international monitoring system and develop on-site inspection procedures.

16. The United Nations has been and is involved in several areas of monitoring and verification. These include investigating prohibited activities through the activities of the United Nations Special Commission (UNSCOM) and the United Nations Monitoring, Verification and Inspection Commission (UNMOVIC) in Iraq; investigating allegations of chemical and biological weapons use through the Secretary-General's mechanism; monitoring the implementation of arms embargoes and sanctions authorized by the Security Council; and monitoring and assisting States in the implementation of obligations such as those arising from Security Council resolution 1540 (2004).

17. The United Nations also facilitates the collection, collation and dissemination of the reports on the confidence-building measures under the Biological and Toxin Weapons Convention; the annual submissions to the Register of Conventional Arms; the annual submissions to the United Nations System for the Standardized Reporting of Military Expenditures; the annual reports required under article 7 of the Convention on the Prohibition of the Use, Stockpiling, Production and Transfer of Anti-personnel Mines and on Their Destruction; data and information, including national reports, on the implementation of the Programme of Action to Prevent, Combat and Eradicate the Illicit Trade in Small Arms and Light Weapons; and reports on confidence-building measures in the field of conventional weapons submitted pursuant to General Assembly resolution 59/92. In addition, the United Nations Institute for Disarmament Research provides information concerning obligations relating to non-proliferation and disarmament treaties, agreements, commitments and their verification.

18. Compliance assessments are an integral element of the verification process. Verification seeks to detect non-compliance, deter would-be non-compliers and build confidence among parties to an agreement. It seeks to detect non-compliance early enough to enable States parties to deal with the situation by bringing the

violator back into compliance; counter the security threat presented by the violation; and thereby deny the violator the benefits of non-compliance. Verification also seeks to enhance transparency and openness, thereby building confidence. Verification thus plays a direct role in contributing to international and national security by providing assurances on the compliance of States with their obligations and commitments.

19. The ability to detect and assess accurately non-compliance depends on factors such as the nature of the obligations, the precision of the language by which they are expressed, the monitoring means included in the agreements, the compliance history of the parties and analytic capabilities. The integration of information from various sources and the degree of access that inspectors have to areas of concern will also be factors. While international bodies may be mandated to verify compliance, ultimate responsibility for making compliance assessments rests with States parties.

20. States have the opportunity to demonstrate their compliance by undertaking confidence-building and transparency measures and providing extra information in addition to the basic legal, mandatory requirements. Conversely, States need to consider that suspicions might arise from their non-participation or partial, reluctant involvement in verification activities.

21. In order for verification to deter States from non-compliance, there need to be clear and assured consequences for non-compliant behaviour. When violations are discovered, the goal is to bring the transgressor back into compliance, consistent with the provisions of the relevant treaty and international law, including the Charter of the United Nations.

22. Non-compliance may be inadvertent or deliberate. In the case of inadvertent non-compliance, States may not be fully aware of their obligations or may misinterpret them. In such cases, advice, encouragement and cooperation, including capacity-building, can help bring States back into compliance and prevent further non-compliance.

23. In cases of deliberate non-compliance constituting a direct challenge to the security of other parties, stronger measures are likely to be necessary. A range of different measures could be applied, in accordance with national legislation and consistent with international law, such as seeking clarifications and assurances through provisions of the relevant treaty, diplomatic and other national, regional and multilateral efforts, and consideration and appropriate action by the Security Council, including measures under Chapters VI and VII of the Charter. Consistency in reacting to situations of non-compliance is important in ensuring widespread support and deterring future non-compliance.

Recommendations for section II

Recommendation 1

24. **Non-proliferation, arms control and disarmament treaties, agreements and commitments, when and if appropriate to the circumstances, should be defined in a way such that they can be subject to effective verification.**

Recommendation 2

25. **Verification approaches should be designed to enable the parties to an agreement to monitor compliance, and detect and collect evidence of possible non-compliance, before that non-compliance threatens the core security objectives of the agreement. To the extent that these objectives can be achieved, it is therefore preferable that treaties, agreements and commitments be supported by an appropriately elaborated set of verification procedures and means that take full account of the nature of the agreement and the relationship among the potential parties.**

Recommendation 3

26. **If it is determined by States that verification cannot be achieved with confidence in this fashion, States may wish to consider proceeding with the agreement using other appropriate means.**

Recommendation 4

27. **Analysis could be undertaken of the capability of existing and possible new verification methods to detect significant, deliberate non-compliance or a pattern of non-compliance with obligations.**

Recommendation 5

28. **Further consideration could be given to responses to withdrawal from treaties where the withdrawing party has misused its technology and technology transfers for peaceful purposes to pursue prohibited weapons-related activities, with specific reference to non-compliance, continuing verification and denying violators the benefits of their violations.**

III. Evolution of the concept of verification since 1995

29. The concept of verification has evolved since 1995. The concept discussed by the Panel included broader elements than traditional verification arrangements. The United Nations, including the Security Council, has played an increasing role in activities, including those related to non-State actors, which fall within the ambit of this broader concept of verification.

30. Cooperative threat reduction activities (for example, the 1991 Nunn-Lugar Cooperative Threat Reduction Program and the Global Partnership against the Spread of Weapons and Materials of Mass Destruction) have produced innovative transparency, reporting and verification measures for assessing implementation and compliance. These agreements have been helpful in building international confidence, including by providing publicly available information on their implementation.

31. Transparency measures such as those found in the Vienna Document, the Open Skies Treaty, the Hague Code of Conduct, the Andean Charter for Peace and Security and the Document on Confidence and Security-Building Measures in the Naval Sphere in the Black Sea have been helpful in building confidence and security.

32. Export controls and export licensing practices for dual-use goods and technologies are becoming increasingly important tools. Advances in tracking and tracing shipments and transfers of dual-use items, including the use of authenticated end-use/user and delivery certificates, are helping in the monitoring of compliance with States' obligations to prohibit illicit transfers of controlled goods and to prevent the proliferation of weapons of mass destruction and their means of delivery.

33. Civil society, including industry, the financial sector, the media, academia and non-governmental organizations, is playing an increasing role in raising awareness of non-proliferation, arms control, disarmament and other obligations and commitments, including those relating to sanctions and arms embargoes, as well as confidence-building measures. It is also acting as a resource for informing individual members of society about the implications of such obligations and commitments. It can also provide resources and expertise to States that may need assistance in national implementation.

34. Arms embargoes and sanctions imposed by the Security Council have been used by the international community to curb the illicit inflow, transfer or acquisition of weapons in certain countries or regions, in the interest of international peace, pressing humanitarian considerations or the prevention of human rights violations. The Security Council relies on Member States, regional and international organizations and its own bodies and mechanisms to monitor the implementation of embargoes and sanctions. Arms embargoes and sanctions work most effectively when all States have the capacity and will to comply with them fully and there is confidence that all States are complying with the obligations they impose. Low-tech monitoring technologies and methodologies are particularly useful in monitoring embargoes and sanctions. In this regard, certain non-governmental organizations and civil society have played an informal role in certain cases in identifying the location of clandestine holdings and illicit transfers of conventional arms.

35. Security Council resolution 1540 (2004) requires all States to implement and enforce the necessary national measures, such as penal and administrative legislation, export controls, and border and customs controls, to prevent the proliferation of nuclear, chemical and biological weapons and their means of delivery. The Security Council, including through its 1540 (2004) Committee, has devised innovative ways to monitor compliance with these obligations, including national reporting. The implementation of resolution 1540 (2004) has revealed a lack of capacity in some States to execute their obligations, even when they are willing to do so. While the 1540 (2004) Committee oversees the implementation of the resolution, there is still a need to assist some States to enable them to be aware of and to meet their obligations.

Recommendations for section III

Recommendation 6

36. **Those in a position to do so might consider assisting relevant States and regional groups in developing the legal, institutional and operational capacity to implement their obligations under Security Council embargoes and sanctions. In this regard, the utilization and continued development of effective, low-tech monitoring technologies and methodologies should be fostered, as well as the strengthening of States' tracking of illegal arms flows and enhanced national controls on imports, exports, financial transactions and brokering relating to illicit arms transfers.**

Recommendation 7

37. **The United Nations could encourage improved coordination among Member States and regional organizations and help affected States to participate actively in monitoring and verifying compliance with arms embargoes and sanctions.**

Recommendation 8

38. **States Members of the United Nations, in line with Security Council resolution 1540 (2004), should consider the kind of practical assistance they can provide, particularly in the areas of reporting and capacity-building, to help States implement their non-proliferation obligations.**

Recommendation 9

39. **Private donors, foundations, non-governmental organizations and international organizations could assist States in ensuring that civil society is aware of its obligations.**

Recommendation 10

40. Partnerships between or among States, the United Nations, other international organizations and civil society to help build capacity for national implementation of States' obligations, including through research and identification of appropriate legislative models and best practices, might be further encouraged, where appropriate.

IV. Verification methods, procedures and technologies

41. Significant developments in verification methods, procedures and technologies have occurred since 1995, serving to increase confidence in the verification process by enhancing flexibility, accuracy, reliability, effectiveness and range. Important practical lessons have been derived from the verification experience.

42. The range of verification techniques and tools has expanded as a result of verification practice and technological developments. Experience has shown that a holistic and multilayered approach is useful to overcome the limitations inherent in individual tools.

43. The availability of improved technologies and methodologies, together with practical experience, has influenced the refinement of existing verification tools and the development of new ones. Verification procedures, such as data mining and interviewing personnel, have proved useful. Advances in data collection, collation, recording and transmission have increased efficiency and reduced costs. States' declarations can now be prepared in electronic format and submitted securely online. Remote monitoring of sensitive facilities is now common practice. The use of satellite observation, aerial overflights — such as those operated under the Open Skies Treaty — and data capture technologies, such as optical cameras, has evolved and is becoming more refined as well as more commonplace.

44. On-site inspection has been enhanced through improvements in observation, sampling, recording and analysis technologies. These include wide-area sampling, portable agent detectors and high-resolution trace analysis that enable minute traces of illicit substances to be detected and identified. Decisions on follow-up measurements and questions can in some instances be made on the spot, enhancing the timeliness, accuracy and cost-effectiveness of inspections.

45. Challenge or special on-site inspections are a potentially useful tool to inspect undeclared sites and facilities. They can increase the risk of detection and the costs of concealing non-compliant activities, and thus may help to deter non-compliance. Such an instrument is found in different verification regimes. For example, it formed an integral part of the confidence- and security-building measures agreed to in the 1986 Stockholm Document for participating States of what was the then Conference on Security and Cooperation in Europe (now OSCE), followed by the Treaty on Conventional Armed Forces in Europe and the Vienna Document 1992. The Chemical Weapons Convention has provisions for short-notice on-site

inspections, anytime and anywhere without the right of refusal. The Comprehensive Nuclear-Test-Ban Treaty, while not in force, contains challenge on-site inspection provisions. IAEA special inspections offer the possibility of inspecting undeclared sites, although it would need the consent of the State concerned for practical implementation. A new development in this area is complementary access under the additional protocol to the safeguards agreements with IAEA. Several bilateral and regional treaties also include provision for challenge inspections. In some agreements and arrangements, challenge inspections are practised frequently as part of the normal confidence-building atmosphere; in others they are treated as highly sensitive instruments and are hardly, if ever, used.

46. Notwithstanding their potential benefits, the degree to which these procedures can help to detect non-compliance depends on the willingness of States to utilize them and the ability to identify locations of concern in a timely manner, to arrive at them before all indications of violation are eliminated and to have sufficient, unimpeded access at those locations, including for sampling, interviewing and document review as appropriate. As a practical matter, there may well be limitations in all these areas and much will depend on circumstances.

47. Technological advances have improved the breadth, availability and quality of information from open sources. A considerable amount of information pertinent to verification is now publicly available on websites, in published form, from commercial sources, including satellites, and from civil society. Data processing has also aided the development of information management systems. For example, integrated data management systems such as those developed by UNMOVIC and used by OPCW can, inter alia, manage State declarations, maps, satellite imagery, on-site inspection reports and sampling reports and provide Intranet, archival and search facilities.

48. International organizations with verification responsibilities have worked together, notably in multidisciplinary teams of inspectors. Cooperation with States has also proved useful to multilateral verification bodies when the provision of information and data from national means has helped the latter to better pinpoint and refine their investigative work in verifying compliance with Security Council resolutions concerning weapons of mass destruction and their means of delivery. For example, satellite imagery and other data have been provided to relevant bodies, including OPCW, IAEA and, in the case of Iraq, UNSCOM/UNMOVIC, by a number of States, as appropriate.

49. There also may be potential for beneficial synergies between verification technology and non-verification applications. For example, the Preparatory Commission for the Comprehensive Nuclear-Test-Ban Treaty Organization is establishing the International Monitoring System, which feeds data into an international data centre for analysis and distribution to member States. Such verification data may also be useful in civil, environmental, disaster management and other scientific applications.

50. In short, one of the most significant changes in verification since the end of the cold war is the growing experience and familiarity of States — and of experts working within States or in international multidisciplinary teams — with verification. For example, bilateral experiences of the United States, the Russian Federation and the Former Soviet Union, the inspections and evaluations conducted bilaterally and multinationally in the Euro-Atlantic region and the experience of the Brazilian-Argentine Agency for Accounting and Control of Nuclear Materials have in their respective ways contributed to a considerable pool of verification knowledge, methods and expertise from which to draw.

51. Regarding the illicit transfer of conventional weapons, there are important challenges for States, particularly related to their tracking of illicit cross-border movement of arms, lack of transparency and reporting, the monitoring of financial activities linked to illicit trafficking and brokering in arms, and appropriate domestic legislation and enforcement capacity.

52. Advances in the availability of low-tech tools, such as aerial and cooperative monitoring, methodologies and synergies, give more States an opportunity to play an active and meaningful role, thereby giving them a greater stake in verification as a means of addressing their security.

Recommendations for section IV

Recommendation 11

53. **States might usefully examine the lessons learned from past verification experiences, including, the use of inspections, interviews, data mining, multidisciplinary approaches, teams and training.**

Recommendation 12

54. **States should consider practically how they might go about handling challenge inspections at sensitive sites in order to manage access in a way that builds confidence that the process can demonstrate compliance, while preventing disclosure of confidential information and data not related to the obligation at hand. This could be done for example through training or table-top exercises and mock inspections with or without involvement of international organizations or other States parties.**

Recommendation 13

55. **There may be scope for further cooperation between and among States and standing verification mechanisms of relevant international organizations to identify potential synergies and collaborative possibilities.**

Recommendation 14

56. Changes in the international security environment can have implications for what States need in their verification toolbox. The creation of new or expanded obligations may require different or new methodologies and techniques (such as, for example, environmental sampling, open-source analysis, interviewing personnel and informal monitoring by civil society). States in a position to do so should continue to research new verification methods and technologies to meet today's challenges and obligations.

Recommendation 15

57. States in a position to do so may wish to consider how best to assist other States in identifying, acquiring and using those verification and monitoring techniques, technologies and methodologies, in particular low-tech, that are best suited to their particular security needs. This could be particularly useful in the area of the illicit transfer of conventional weapons.

V. Verification and compliance mechanisms

58. Responsibility to improve verification and compliance mechanisms lies, quite properly, with the States that have undertaken treaty obligations, freely committed themselves to constraints in armaments and to disarmament activities, or have been obligated by Security Council resolutions. States acting collectively in their capacity as members of a particular treaty or regime, and subject to their internal ratification procedures, have the authority to change, improve and deepen verification or introduce new methods, technologies and measures for that regime.

59. One mechanism comes directly under the auspices of the United Nations — that is, the Secretary-General's mechanism, which is an important potential tool for investigating and verifying the possible use of chemical or biological weapons.

60. By its resolution 42/37 C, the General Assembly requested the Secretary-General to establish a mechanism to investigate the alleged use of chemical or biological weapons, and in that context requested him to further develop technical guidelines and procedures for such investigations, and to compile and maintain a list of relevant experts and laboratories. Following the adoption of Security Council resolution 620 (1988), the Assembly, by resolution 45/57 C, endorsed the ensuing proposals to operationalize the mechanism, including those authorizing the Secretary-General to update it periodically. This mechanism has not been updated as a whole since 1989, although there has been some revision of the list of experts and laboratories. It is unclear whether it would now be able to work effectively if the Secretary-General were called upon to investigate allegations of chemical or biological weapons use. There have been no exercises or operational/logistical planning to ensure that the Secretary-General could in fact send an investigative team of highly trained inspectors in a moment of crisis or need.

61. Standing detailed procedures for the investigation of alleged chemical weapons use have been developed by OPCW for States parties to the Chemical Weapons Convention since 1997. The United Nations and OPCW subsequently concluded an agreement whereby the Secretary-General of the United Nations may request OPCW to investigate alleged use by States not parties to the Convention or territories not controlled by States parties (see General Assembly resolution 55/283).

62. States individually and on a regional basis, as well as OPCW and other international organizations, have taken and are taking steps to improve their ability to investigate chemical and biological weapons use. The Panel has considered the value of taking advantage of existing and planned national and regional capabilities and synergies and greater coordination among international organizations with a view to avoiding unnecessary duplication of effort.

63. Ever-increasing obligations have increased reporting requirements. Some States have difficulties in coping with the reporting burden. Simplification of reporting forms and electronic formats have gone some way in reducing the burden. At the same time, increased reporting requirements have provided more information from States that needs to be collated, disseminated, analysed and verified. Much of the information required is available from open sources, such as the Internet and published government reports, but there are constraints on the capacity of the United Nations to gather and process such information.

64. Regional and bilateral arrangements and organizations can play a role in promoting compliance and detecting non-compliance. Such bodies include regional organizations involved in implementing and monitoring compliance with nuclear-weapon-free zone agreements; and bilateral bodies such as those established by the various United States/Russian Federation nuclear arms control agreements, as well as the Brazilian-Argentine Agency for Accounting and Control of Nuclear Materials and the European Atomic Energy Community. They may also be especially useful in investigating suspicious activities within their region, such as outbreaks of infectious disease or attempts to procure materials or components related to weapons of mass destruction. The authority under which such regional bodies or groups of States act may be provided by Security Council resolutions or through regional agreements.

65. Finally, with a few exceptions, multilateral and regional verification and implementation organizations have to date cooperated only sporadically, despite having formal agreements that permit and encourage cooperation. Part of this is due to their different mandates and responsibilities. As improvements continue in monitoring and remote-sensing technologies, data-gathering and processing, environmental techniques and so forth, there is greater scope for one organization's work to be of use to another, even if the specific mandates are different.

Recommendations for section V

Recommendation 16

66. In the context of General Assembly resolutions 42/37 C and 45/57 C, States could consider ways in which they could contribute to making the Secretary-General's mechanism to investigate alleged use of chemical or biological weapons more operational and cost-effective through national measures.

Recommendation 17

67. Consideration should be given to strengthening ties and establishing appropriate standing arrangements with international organizations, including OPCW, States and regional bodies, so as to build upon and make use of their relevant investigative capabilities and make the mechanism more operational and cost-effective.

Recommendation 18

68. States that have not done so should consider providing the names of experts and/or laboratories to facilitate the updating of the relevant lists.

Recommendation 19

69. States could continue to explore the synergies that may exist in the area of techniques and methodologies of monitoring and verification and in addressing situations relating to compliance and non-compliance.

Recommendation 20

70. International organizations mandated to collect information from States in support of monitoring States' compliance with obligations might consider ways and means of alleviating or mitigating the overlap, as well as of improving the ways in which data are collected and disseminated to States.

Recommendation 21

71. Bilateral and regional arrangements could be encouraged to play a role, where appropriate, in promoting compliance, building confidence and detecting, assessing and responding to non-compliance.

VI. Final recommendation

72. The panel recommends that States Members of the United Nations give active consideration to the recommendations of this report and to how they might, acting singly or in concert with other States, take up any of the recommendations for development. They could also be subject to further consideration under the respective treaties or by the appropriate United Nations body or group.

Part 2

Background material

I. General Assembly resolutions and note

A. A/RES/62/21 (which commends the report to the attention of Member States)

Verification in all its aspects, including the role of the United Nations in the field of verification

The General Assembly,

Recalling its resolution 59/60 of 3 December 2004, in which it requested the Secretary-General, with the assistance of a panel of government experts, to explore the question of verification in all its aspects, including the role of the United Nations in the field of verification,

Noting two previous reports of the Secretary-General on the subject submitted in 1990 and 1995,[1]

Recalling its request to the Secretary-General, in resolution 59/60, to transmit to it the report of the Panel of Government Experts on verification in all its aspects, including the role of the United Nations in the field of verification, and the intent of the Panel to produce a report that is forward-looking and discerning of new trends and requirements,

1. *Takes note* of the report of the Panel of Government Experts on verification in all its aspects, including the role of the United Nations in the field of verification,[2] transmitted by the Secretary-General on 15 August 2007, acknowledges that the report was unanimously approved by the Panel of Government Experts, and commends the report to the attention of Member States;

2. *Requests* the Secretary-General to give the report the widest possible circulation;

---

[1] A/45/372 and Corr.1 and A/50/377 and Corr.1.
[2] A/61/1028.

3. *Encourages* Member States to consider the report, and invites Member States to offer additional views to the Secretary-General on the report;

4. *Requests* the Secretary-General to submit to the General Assembly at its sixty-third session a compilation of views received from Member States, relevant United Nations organs and international treaty organizations with respect to the report;

5. *Decides* to include in the provisional agenda of its sixty-fourth session the item entitled "Verification in all its aspects, including the role of the United Nations in the field of verification".

61st plenary meeting
5 December 2007

B. Note of the General Assembly of 8 December 2005

At its 61st plenary meeting on 8 December 2005, the General Assembly took note of the report of the First Committee.*

C. A/RES/59/60 (which called for views of Member States and set up the Panel of Experts)

Verification in all its aspects, including the role of the United Nations in the field of verification

The General Assembly,

Noting the critical importance of and the vital contribution that has been made by effective verification measures in non-proliferation, arms limitation and disarmament agreements and other similar obligations,

Reaffirming its support for the sixteen principles of verification drawn up by the Disarmament Commission,[1]

Recalling its resolutions 40/152 O of 16 December 1985, 41/86 Q of 4 December 1986, 42/42 F of 30 November 1987, 43/81 B of 7 December 1988, 45/65 of 4 December 1990, 47/45 of 9 December 1992, 48/68 of 16 December 1993, 50/61 of 12 December 1995, 52/31 of 9 December 1997, 54/46 of

---

* The report of the First Committee, A/60/458, states that the Committee had before it the report of the Secretary-General on verification in all its aspects, including the role of the United Nations in the field of verification (A/60/96) and informs that "no proposals were submitted and no action was taken by the Committee under this item". A/60/96 of 5 July 2005 contains the views of Member States collected in 2005 and 2006 on the issue (see p. 27).

[1] See *Official Records of the General Assembly, Fifteenth Special Session, Supplement No. 3* (A/S-15/3), para. 60 (para. 6, sect. I, of the quoted text).

1 December 1999 and 56/15 of 29 November 2001, as well as its decision 58/515 of 8 December 2003,

Recalling also the reports of the Secretary-General of 11 July 1986, 28 August 1990, 16 September 1992, 26 July 1993, 22 September 1995, 6 August 1997, 9 July 1999, 10 September 2001 and 10 July 2003, and the addenda thereto,[2]

1. *Reaffirms* the critical importance of and the vital contribution that has been made by effective verification measures in non-proliferation, arms limitation and disarmament agreements and other similar obligations;

2. *Requests* the Secretary-General to report to the General Assembly at its sixtieth session on further views received from Member States;

3. *Also requests* the Secretary-General, with the assistance of a panel of government experts to be established in 2006 on the basis of equitable geographic distribution, to explore the question of verification in all its aspects, including the role of the United Nations in the field of verification, and to transmit the report of the panel of experts to the General Assembly for consideration at its sixty-first session;

4. *Decides* to include in the provisional agenda of its sixty-first session the item entitled "Verification in all its aspects, including the role of the United Nations in the field of verification".

66th plenary meeting
3 December 2004

II. Sixteen Principles of Verification*

Adopted by the United Nations Disarmament Commission and commended by the General Assembly in resolution A/43/78 A

1. Adequate and effective verification is an essential element of all arms limitation and disarmament agreements.

2. Verification is not an aim in itself, but an essential element in the process of achieving arms limitation and disarmament agreements.

3. Verification should promote the implementation of arms limitation and disarmament measures, build confidence among States and ensure that agreements are being observed by all parties.

---

[2] A/41/422 and Add.1 and 2, A/45/372 and Corr.1, A/47/405 and Add.1, A/48/227 and Add.1 and 2, A/50/377 and Corr.1, A/52/269, A/54/166, A/56/347 and Add.1 and A/58/128.

* See *Official Records of the General Assembly, Fifteenth Special Session, Supplement No. 3* (A/S-15/3), para. 60 (para. 6, sect. I, of the quoted text), 28 May 1988.

4. Adequate and effective verification requires employment of different techniques, such as national technical means, international technical means and international procedures, including on-site inspections.

5. Verification in the arms limitation and disarmament process will benefit from greater openness.

6. Arms limitation and disarmament agreements should include explicit provisions whereby each party undertakes not to interfere with the agreed methods, procedures and techniques of verification, when these are operating in a manner consistent with the provisions of the agreement and generally recognized principles of international law.

7. Arms limitation and disarmament agreements should include explicit provisions whereby each party undertakes not to use deliberate concealment measures which impede verification of compliance with the agreement.

8. To assess the continuing adequacy and effectiveness of the verification system, an arms limitation and disarmament agreement should provide for procedures and mechanisms for review and evaluation. Where possible, time frames for such reviews should be agreed in order to facilitate this assessment.

9. Verification arrangements should be addressed at the outset and at every stage of negotiations on specific arms limitation and disarmament agreements.

10. All States have equal rights to participate in the process of international verification of agreements to which they are parties.

11. Adequate and effective verification arrangements must be capable of providing, in a timely fashion, clear and convincing evidence of compliance or non-compliance. Continued confirmation of compliance is an essential ingredient to building and maintaining confidence among the parties.

12. Determinations about the adequacy, effectiveness and acceptability of specific methods and arrangements intended to verify compliance with the provisions of an arms limitation and disarmament agreement can only be made within the context of that agreement.

13. Verification of compliance with the obligations imposed by an arms limitation and disarmament agreement is an activity conducted by the parties to an arms limitation and disarmament agreement or by an organization at the request and with the explicit consent of the parties, and is an expression of the sovereign right of States to enter into such arrangements.

14. Requests for inspections or information in accordance with the provisions of an arms limitation and disarmament agreement should be considered as a normal component of the verification process. Such requests should be used only for the purposes of the determination of compliance, care being taken to avoid abuses.

15. Verification arrangements should be implemented without discrimination, and, in accomplishing their purpose, avoid unduly interfering with the internal affairs of State parties or other States, or jeopardizing their economic, technological and social development.

16. To be adequate and effective, a verification regime for an agreement must cover all relevant weapons, facilities, locations, installations and activities.

III. Views of Member States (excerpted from A/60/96 and Add.1 and 2)

The following are the views presented by Member States in pursuance of paragraph 2 of resolution A/59/60, entitled "Verification in all its aspects, including the role of the United Nations in the field of verification", adopted on 3 December 2004.

Bolivia

[Original: Spanish]
[5 April 2006]

General Assembly resolution 59/60 of 3 December 2004 reaffirms the critical importance of and the vital contribution that has been made by effective verification measures in non-proliferation, arms limitation and disarmament agreements and other similar obligations.

Bolivia considers that the most effective mechanism for ensuring non-proliferation, arms limitation and disarmament is verification of compliance by States parties with their commitments.

The role of the United Nations in verification activities is vital in order to build the necessary level of confidence within the international community.

Bolivia believes that dialogue and negotiation are the best means of resolving disputes.

Moreover, given the current threats to the international system, arms control and verification is crucial in combating terrorism and transnational organized crime.

In keeping with its pacifist policy and with the global initiative for disarmament and non-proliferation, Bolivia supports the work of the international agencies of the United Nations system to promote disarmament and the peaceful uses of nuclear energy with a view to ensuring international peace and security.

Canada

[Original: English]
[18 May 2005]

The following paper provides the views of Canada on the implementation of General Assembly resolution 59/60, by which the Assembly decided to establish a panel of government experts in 2006 mandated to examine verification in all of its aspects, including the role of the United Nations. It examines the international security context for verification, work completed on verification issues by previous United Nations expert groups and current Canadian perspectives on verification. This paper concludes with a brief discussion of a number of considerations regarding the proposed work of the 2006 panel of government experts.

Verification and international security

Verified compliance with arms control and disarmament agreements provides significant security benefits to the international community. These benefits are as important today as they were during the cold war. We must continue to "trust but verify" precisely because non-compliance with freely negotiated arms control and disarmament agreements can seriously erode the trust so vital to the success of such agreements.

While verification mechanisms do require a commitment of resources, these resources are widely recognized as wise investments when compared to the costs of alternative security approaches such as the maintenance of large conventional forces or stockpiles of nuclear, chemical or biological weapons. Moreover, the continued existence of weapons of mass destruction (WMD) and the threat they constitute to international peace and security, argue that potential non-compliance with WMD disarmament and non-proliferation obligations will remain a critical issue of war and peace for the foreseeable future.

Verification and the United Nations

The United Nations has long recognized the value of verification. The first United Nations special session on disarmament in 1978 noted in its Declaration that "Disarmament and arms limitation agreements should provide for adequate measures of verification satisfactory to all parties concerned in order to create the necessary confidence and ensure that they are being observed by all parties."[*]

In December 1985, the General Assembly adopted resolution 40/152 O "Verification in all its aspects" by consensus. The resolution, initiated by Canada, called upon States, inter alia, to communicate to the Secretary-General their views on verification principles, procedures and techniques to promote the inclusion of adequate verification in arms limitation and disarmament agreements, and on the role of the United Nations in the field of verification.

---

[*] A/RES/S-10/2, para. 31.

In 1988, the General Assembly endorsed a set of 16 principles of verification developed by the United Nations Disarmament Commission, which continue to enjoy support through biennial resolutions of the Assembly. The central role of verification was reflected in the first of these 16 principles, which states that "Adequate and effective verification is an essential element of all arms limitation and disarmament agreements".

Building upon this early work, the General Assembly requested the Secretary-General to undertake, with the assistance of a group of governmental experts, a detailed study of the role of the United Nations in the field of verification. The report of the Group of Experts was submitted to the Assembly in 1990. In its resolution 45/65 the Assembly welcomed the report and requested the Secretary-General to take appropriate follow-up action. The 1990 Group of Experts offered conclusions and recommendations in six main areas related to the role of the United Nations in the field of verification:

1. Data-collection capability;
2. Exchanges between experts and diplomats;
3. Role of the Secretary-General in fact finding and other activities;
4. Use of aircraft for verification purposes;
5. Use of satellites;
6. An international verification system.

In the light of the rapidly changing nature of disarmament and international security in the immediate post-cold war era, General Assembly resolution 48/68 of 16 December 1993 once again established a group of governmental experts to examine "the lessons of recent United Nations verification experience and other relevant international developments and to explore the further development of guidelines and principles for the involvement of the United Nations in verification". The 1995 Group of Experts provided recommendations on possible roles for the United Nations in three areas:

1. Facilitating and coordinating roles between existing verification procedures and implementing bodies;
2. Common service roles, including provisions of databases, information collection and analysis, and training and involving the development of expertise within the United Nations upon which other organizations, other parts of the United Nations or Member States can draw to meet verification requirements; and

3. Operational roles related to third-party verification and specific obligations that require verification, for which the United Nations has responsibility. *

Some of the recommendations provided by these earlier Group of Expert efforts have been implemented at the national or international level, but several have not yet been fully considered or acted upon.

Canadian perspectives on verification

The recent interest of Canada in verification issues can be traced to its 1986 study entitled "Verification in All its Aspects: A Comprehensive Study on Arms Control and Disarmament Verification Pursuant to General Assembly resolution 40/152 O". Through its verification research programme, Canada has undertaken a broad range of verification research efforts since the mid-1980s, including weapons-specific as well as cross-sector and interdisciplinary studies. Canada played an active role in the development of the 16 principles of verification and had the honour of chairing the 1995 Group of Government Experts mandated to examine verification in all its aspects. Noting the continued importance of verification within the new international security context, Canada initiated a discussion of verification issues in the First Committee at the fifty-eighth session of the General Assembly. In October 2004, Canada submitted a revised version of its biennial verification resolution, adopted without a vote, which solicited views of Member States on the issue of verification in all its aspects and the United Nations role therein and agreed to establish a Panel of Government Experts to convene in 2006 and report back to the General Assembly.

Canada also continues its tradition of funding advanced verification research through its International Security Research and Outreach Programme (ISROP) within Foreign Affairs Canada. In anticipation of the convening of the 2006 panel of government experts, as well as to support the work of the Weapons of Mass Destruction Commission (Blix Commission), Canada commissioned a two-part study through ISROP in the fall of 2004 designed to update our thinking on verification issues. The first part of the study entitled "WMD verification and compliance: the state of play" (October 2004) was completed for ISROP by the United Kingdom-based Verification Research, Training and Information Centre (VERTIC). The report was designed to provide an updated baseline analysis of the principal WMD agreements and the mechanisms by which compliance with their obligations is verified and, when required, suspected and verified non-compliance issues are resolved. A copy of the report can be found on the website of the Weapons of Mass Destruction Commission at http://www.wmdcommission.org/files/No19.pdf.

Building on the VERTIC analysis, a second report, entitled "Weapons of Mass Destruction Verification and Compliance: Challenges and Responses" (November

---

* A/50/377, p. 10.

2004), was commissioned from 59 Canadian and international experts. It attempted to address two forward-looking questions: what are the challenges currently facing our WMD verification and compliance mechanisms, and what are some of the practical and potentially achievable responses to these challenges? This study utilized an integrated consultation process which combined an Internet-based expert questionnaire containing 72 questions on WMD-related verification and compliance issues, followed by a series of five conference calls and a two-day workshop with approximately 20 Canadian and international Government and non-government experts. A copy of the report can be found on the website of the Weapons of Mass Destruction Commission at http://www.wmdcommission.org/files/No20.pdf.

The second report included a total of 39 specific verification and compliance related recommendations, presented to the Weapons of Mass Destruction Commission in November 2004, within four main thematic areas:

1. Expanding the scope of WMD verification and compliance mechanisms;
2. Addressing emerging verification challenges;
3. Compliance management;
4. Investing in smart WMD verification and compliance mechanisms.

The aim of this most recent Canadian verification research effort was not to reach specific conclusions on these issues, and its results do not reflect official Canadian Government policy. Rather it was designed to draw upon the views of a relatively large group of experts to stimulate substantive examination of verification and compliance challenges currently facing the multilateral community. The two reports in fact reveal an active and very rich international debate on these issues and, as such, may prove useful as a background to further consideration by States or by the Panel of Experts.

Considerations regarding the work of the 2006 panel of government experts

International developments and the views provided by the experts consulted by Canada during the development of its research submission to the Weapons of Mass Destruction Commission suggest there is important work that could be usefully undertaken by the 2006 United Nations panel of government experts in at least four main areas.

1. **Review of the conclusions of the 1995 Group of Experts.** Consistent with the approach of earlier expert groups, Canada would like the work of the 2006 panel of government experts to begin with a review of previous United Nations work, especially the report of the 1995 Group of Experts. This effort should focus on the identification of areas of analysis that could be usefully updated in order to provide a longer-term vision of key trends within the verification sector. In order to advance the work of the 2006 panel, consideration should be given to asking an expert consultant to complete baseline analysis prior to the first meeting of the panel. This

analysis should include a review of more recent work undertaken within the United Nations context on verification issues, such as the recommendations of the Secretary-General's Advisory Board on Disarmament Matters, the High-Level Panel on Threats, Challenges and Change, and the recent report of the Secretary-General "In larger freedom: towards development, security and human rights for all". There are also a number of expert studies relevant to verification issues that have been produced outside the United Nations context that could provide useful information for this analysis.

2. **Lessons from recent verification experiences**. Much has happened since the 1995 Group of Government Experts completed its work, and a great deal can and should be learned from practical verification experiences over the past decade. Among other aspects, the report "WMD verification and compliance: the state of play" suggests that WMD verification institutions, techniques and technologies have evolved dramatically over the past few years. In this regard, the growing technical competence of international verification bodies such as the International Atomic Energy Agency, the Organization for the Prohibition of Chemical Weapons and the Comprehensive Nuclear-Test-Ban Treaty Organization is widely recognized. Approaches in the conventional arms sector can also provide valuable, often innovative, experience on which to draw, in areas such as the contribution of non-governmental organizations in monitoring treaty implementation, a role played by the *Landmine Monitor* with regard to the Convention on the Prohibition of the Use, Stockpiling, Production and Transfer of Anti-Personnel Mines and on Their Destruction (the Mine Ban Treaty).

3. **Improvements in existing mechanisms**. Some verification mechanisms still need to be universalized, and this must remain a priority. Other mechanisms need to be improved or more fully implemented. The need for technical improvements in the light of new technologies, techniques and challenges presented by the new security environment requires examination, including the contribution that new scientific and technical developments can make to improve verification. Rapid scientific developments, however, require attention in that they can produce new or modified weapons and new ways to disguise the development of such new weapons. The issue of the acquisition and use of WMD by non-State actors has also emerged as a major issue of concern in recent years, given that most of our verification mechanisms were initially developed to address State-to-State security concerns.

4. **The role of the United Nations in the field of verification**. There is widespread recognition that there are significant gaps within the current international verification system and there has been an active debate about what role the United Nations might play in addressing these important capability gaps.

The need for some form of verification regime to address biological weapons issues remains a significant concern. The 2006 panel of experts could explore ways to address this lacuna in ways that complement ongoing efforts to strengthen the Convention on the Prohibition of the Development, Production and Stockpiling of

Bacteriological (Biological) and Toxin Weapons and on Their Destruction itself. The investigative mechanism of the Secretary-General regarding the alleged use of biological and chemical weapons also requires updating as the lists of available personnel are considerably out of date.

There is also a pressing need to address verification issues associated with WMD delivery systems, such as ballistic or cruise missiles or unmanned aerial vehicles. It is true that such systems are not currently constrained by any multilateral legally binding control regime upon which verification mechanisms could be based. Useful work should, however, still be undertaken on missile verification recognizing, inter alia, the fact that the United Nations has already been called upon by the Security Council, through the United Nations Monitoring, Verification and Inspection Commission (UNMOVIC) to conduct ballistic missile verification efforts.

Related to the potential proliferation of WMD to non-State actors, Security Council resolution 1540 (2004) presents new verification challenges that could be usefully addressed by the panel of experts. If resolution 1540 (2004) is to become an effective mechanism through which to address the implementation of WMD prohibitions at the national level, there is a clear need for the completeness and accuracy of the national submissions provided to the United Nations pursuant to this resolution to be effectively verified as a critical step towards addressing compliance issues.

Beyond WMD issues, there are also important questions related to roles the United Nations might play in verifying compliance with conventional arms embargoes or other restrictions on conventional arms imposed by the Security Council or otherwise agreed by Member States. For example, the Secretary-General is the depository for the 1997 Mine Ban Treaty and plays a central role in the verification mechanisms negotiated for that regime. The 1980 Convention on Prohibitions or Restrictions on the Use of Certain Conventional Weapons which May be Deemed to be Excessively Injurious or to Have Indiscriminate Effects continues to expand into new areas and is in the process of considering appropriate compliance mechanisms. The panel of experts could also examine the role of the United Nations in verification efforts associated with the implementation of disarmament obligations associated with local agreements such as peace support operations.

There are also critical issues associated with the development of the institutional capacity of the United Nations to support verification, including the relationship of such capacity to other international verification institutions. In this regard, the experience with UNMOVIC has clearly demonstrated the capability of the United Nations to develop and maintain a highly professional, impartial and effective verification organization capable of operating in even the most difficult political environments. The UNMOVIC experience also underscores the tremendous synergies that can be realized through genuine cooperation and complementarity between the United Nations and the specialized agencies such as the International Atomic Energy Agency and the Organization for the Prohibition of Chemical Weapons.

At least two key institutional lessons from the United Nations experience of the past decade appear to be clear and directly relevant to the issue of United Nations verification capabilities. It is very difficult to develop new United Nations capacities rapidly in response to urgent requirements. It is equally clear that once such capacities have been developed, caution should be exercised regarding decisions to abandon them. One important task for the 2006 panel of experts should be the careful evaluation of the merits of a standing United Nations verification capacity, drawing on the lessons learned from the UNMOVIC experience. It is noteworthy in this regard that the issue of a standing multilateral verification capability has been actively considered by previous verification expert groups. The 2006 panel of experts should consider if this is an idea whose time has finally come.

Chile

[Original: Spanish]
[13 May 2005]

Chile considers that all disarmament instruments should establish effective verification measures, since verification is the mechanism that allows for maximum security that nuclear, chemical and biological materials and facilities are being used solely for peaceful purposes. An effective safeguards system acts as a confidence-building measure, an early-warning mechanism and a trigger for preventive action by the international community against non-peaceful use.

Chile has concluded an additional protocol to its agreement on the application of safeguards with the International Atomic Energy Agency (IAEA) and is in favour of the adoption of such a protocol by all States.

Chile is a party to the Comprehensive Nuclear-Test-Ban Treaty and participates in its verification system through seven monitoring stations using the four technologies. It is currently considering the installation of an eighth ultrasound station. Chile has regularly urged the States whose adherence to the Treaty is required for its entry into force to sign and ratify it.

Chile considers that the Annex on Implementation and Verification of the Convention on the Prohibition of the Development, Production, Stockpiling and Use of Chemical Weapons and on Their Destruction has been important in verifying the destruction of chemical weapons by the States parties possessing them and in establishing controls on the international chemical industry with regard to the production of dual-use substances. However, it believes that States possessing chemical weapons should proceed more quickly towards completing their planned destruction by 2012.

In Chile a bill is under consideration to amend Act No. 17,798 on arms control; the bill would empower the Ministry of Defence to monitor and control items having to do with chemicals, industrial facilities, laboratories and installations intended for the stockpiling, storage, use, production or processing of chemicals or their precursors subject to control under the international treaties to which Chile is a party, and items used in the physical and chemical processes.

Chile has played an active role in international forums in the search for consensus formulas that would allow for progress in the adoption of a verification mechanism for the Convention on the Prohibition of the Development, Production and Stockpiling of Bacteriological (Biological) and Toxin Weapons and on Their Destruction.

Chile is also a party and has played an active role in relation to the Convention on Prohibitions or Restrictions on the Use of Certain Conventional Weapons Which May Be Deemed to Be Excessively Injurious or to Have Indiscriminate Effects; the Convention on the Prohibition of the Use, Stockpiling, Production and Transfer of Anti-Personnel Mines and on Their Destruction; and the International Code of Conduct against Ballistic Missile Proliferation.

Cuba

[Original: Spanish]
[23 June 2006]

The Republic of Cuba considers that verification is a vitally important process that helps to foster the necessary confidence in relations between States and to gauge compliance with non-proliferation, arms limitation, arms control and disarmament agreements.

Any disarmament agreement that provides for practical verification measures must be preceded by a formal undertaking by the States parties to refrain completely from the threat or use of force, whether exercised unilaterally or on the basis of an alliance, irrespective of whether such an undertaking forms part of their other international obligations.

The verification process should uphold the principle of confidentiality, be minimally intrusive and respect, and in no case endanger, the national security of States. Verification should also be objective and transparent. All States should receive the same treatment.

Cuba considers that every disarmament agreement should establish its own verification system and place particular emphasis on measures for consultation, cooperation and clarification of doubts.

Nothing should limit the right of States parties to comment and vote on issues that directly or indirectly concern them. Verification should be based on non-discriminatory and non-selective principles. All States have the same right to participate in the verification processes established under the agreements to which they are parties.

Verification is not an end in itself, but a means of ensuring that all parties comply with agreements.

As part of disarmament agreements, verification measures should apply only to those States that are parties to such agreements, and should in no case affect other States.

The verification system established under the Convention on Chemical Weapons and the verification measures employed by the International Atomic Energy Agency (IAEA) may be used as a basis for other disarmament agreements.

The Republic of Cuba reaffirms its support for the 16 principles of verification drawn up by the United Nations Disarmament Commission (General Assembly resolution 43/81 B).

The Republic of Cuba reiterates that verification agreements should be applied without discrimination and in a manner that avoids any undue interference in the internal affairs of States parties and any impediment to the full exercise by all States of the right to social and economic development and access to technology.

Finland

[Original: English]
[28 April 2006]

Finland attaches great importance to verification in the field of disarmament, arms control and non-proliferation and supports the enhancement of verification-related capacities of the United Nations. As new threats to disarmament regimes emerge and new means to verify compliance become available, an international discussion on verification, in all its aspects, becomes even more necessary.

A number of useful contributions from Member States towards the work of the 2006 Panel of Governmental Experts on this subject have already been made. To support the work of the Panel, Finland would like to offer the following additional comments and looks forward to the publication of the Panel's results and the subsequent discussion at the United Nations.

Existing verification arrangements in the field of disarmament and non-proliferation leave significant lacunae to be filled by new efforts of the international community. Besides the weakness of verification tools in the Biological and Toxin Weapons Convention and slow progress with the entry into force of the Comprehensive Nuclear-Test-Ban Treaty, fissile materials and missiles lack a regime and thus also verification arrangements. Verification also remains a challenge in the field of conventional weapons. These shortfalls should be addressed through relevant treaty regimes but also through strengthening the verification capacities of the United Nations, especially the Secretary-General.

For reasons of effectiveness, Finland considers it important that future strengthening of United Nations verification capacities make full use of expertise gathered, methods developed and lessons learned in past and ongoing United Nations verification work, in particular that of the United Nations Monitoring, Verification and Inspection Commission. Existing resources — roster of trained experts, Headquarters staff, recruitment and training system, investigation methods as well as data collection and management tools — should not be lost. That requires action at the level of the United Nations but also nationally in its Member States.

One existing United Nations mechanism that should be built upon is the investigative mechanism of the Secretary-General regarding the alleged use of biological and chemical weapons. Member States should maintain and regularly update the lists of experts and laboratories that they have notified to the mechanism, and the Department for Disarmament Affairs secretariat should regularly remind Member States of that duty. Preparations should also be launched with a view to enhancing the working procedures of the mechanism.

To ensure effectiveness, reliability, credibility and legitimacy for United Nations verification work, it is important that experts nominated to the Secretary-General mechanism as well as other personnel involved in United Nations verification work be highly professional and competent. Training and exercises are important tools for enhancing and maintaining necessary skills. Legitimacy of verification arrangements also depends on jointly agreed and transparent investigation procedures as well as scientifically validated investigation techniques, equipment and tests. These, in turn, call for promotion of international laboratory networks and exchange of scientists. Finally, United Nations verification work should follow relevant scientific and technical developments and make use of new capacities such as mobile field laboratories.

Finland considers it important that the United Nations take into account ongoing verification-related work, experience gained and lessons learned in other international organizations, such as the Organization for the Prohibition of Chemical Weapons (OPCW) and the International Atomic Energy Agency. On the chemical weapons side, the Secretary-General should liaise with the OPCW to benefit from the lessons it has learned from its regular industry inspections, maintaining capacity for the so-called challenge inspections and exercising procedures in cases of alleged use. The role and potential of the OPCW-designated laboratories network should also be considered. As regards biological weapons, the strengthening of United Nations verification capacities should take into account any future developments in the Biological and Toxin Weapons Convention. Networking with other relevant international organizations, in particular the World Health Organization, should also be carefully examined.

Several arms control and disarmament agreements, commitments and arrangements include provisions on confidence-building measures or other information exchange, such as reporting for the Committee established under Security Council resolution 1540 (2004). Finland views these exchanges as an important element of verification regimes, both of conventional and non-conventional weapons, and emphasizes the importance of timely, accurate and comprehensive participation. In addition to information exchange among States parties, Finland underlines the importance of transparency and public information more generally. Transparency concerning the implementation of arms control and disarmament commitments provides the public with an opportunity to contribute to verification and should also strengthen public support to arms control, disarmament and non-proliferation efforts.

Guatemala

[Original: Spanish]
[9 May 2005]

I have the honour to transmit below the information requested.

A. The State of Guatemala, at the regional level, as party to the Central American Integration System, is involved in setting the schedule for the programme for arms limitation and control in Central America to achieve a reasonable balance of forces and to foster stability, mutual trust and transparency.

B. In 2006 it would be helpful if the official assigned to the Conference of Armed Forces of Central America were to be involved in exploring the question of verification, including the role of the United Nations in the field of verification, called for in paragraph 3 of General Assembly resolution 59/60.

Islamic Republic of Iran

[Original: English]
[28 December 2005]

The attainment of the objective of security, as an inseparable element of peace, has always been one of the most profound aspirations of the international community, which has adopted different measures, to advance this objective. The General Assembly, in the Final Document of the Tenth Special Session, devoted to disarmament, recognized that "among such measures, effective measures of nuclear disarmament and the prevention of nuclear war have the highest priority".[*] The Assembly further agreed that "in order to facilitate the conclusion and effective

---

[*] Resolution S-10/2, para. 20.

implementation of disarmament agreements and to create confidence, States should accept appropriate provisions for verification in such agreements".*

In addition to the general principles elaborated in the Final Document, the Disarmament Commission agreed, by consensus, on the sixteen principles related to verification, which were the result of long and painstaking deliberations.** The panel of government experts, to be established in 2006 on the basis of equitable geographic distribution, will be entrusted with further exploring the work of the Commission and its sixteen principles of verification. In our opinion, the success of the panel greatly depends on taking stock of the different views of all States on the above-mentioned principles.

The Islamic Republic of Iran believes that the work of the panel on the question of verification in all its aspects should be based on the principles already agreed in the Final Document of the Tenth Special Session and by the Disarmament Commission.

We concur with the view that verification is not an aim in itself, and that it is only an important and an integral part of all arms control and disarmament agreements and is aimed at building confidence and ensuring the observance of agreements by all parties. Verification provisions of disarmament agreements need to be carefully drafted in order to ensure the interests and concerns of respective parties. Verification procedures may include intrusive arrangements such as on-site inspection. In such a case, any abuse or interference beyond agreed verification procedures should be avoided. Verification is not an element independent from other aspects of agreements. Therefore, it can not be implemented without due regard for the other aspects of the respective agreements.

Verification activities by the concerned parties or by an organization should be conducted at the request of and with the explicit consent of the parties.

In the view of the Islamic Republic of Iran, once agreement is reached on the verification provisions by all parties and implemented by the competent authority or concerned parties, all States parties to such an agreement should abide by the result of verification and refrain from making unsubstantiated allegations or resorting to unilateral actions.

Funding of the verification activities and the techniques and technologies used in verification processes in accordance with the provisions of the relevant agreement are of great importance, which need to be elaborated in detail, either in the negotiation phase or in the implementation process, as has been the case in the Organization for the Prohibition of Chemical Weapons.

Avoiding duplication of the work by various bodies and specialized agencies engaging in the field of verification such as the International Atomic Energy

---

* Ibid., para. 91.
** See A/51/182, section G, part I.

Agency, the Organization for the Prohibition of Chemical Weapons and the Comprehensive Nuclear-Test-Ban Treaty Organization is imperative. It is therefore wise to invite those bodies to share their experience in the field of verification, in a proper manner. At the request of and with the explicit consent of the parties to an agreement, the United Nations could also have a role in the field of verification for such an agreement. The credibility of the work of the panel also depends on the appropriate political representation in its membership.

The Islamic Republic of Iran attaches great importance to the issue of verification in all its aspects and looks forward to an in-depth discussion in this regard within the framework of the United Nations.

Japan

[Original: English]
[20 April 2005]

Japan attaches great importance to the verification in the field of arms control, disarmament and non-proliferation.

With regard to the proposal of establishing a panel of government experts in 2006, Japan considers it important to set clear guidance for the objectives and the scope of the discussion at the panel before its establishment.

It should be pointed out that there are various aspects to be considered. First, we already have the verification system of the International Atomic Energy Agency (IAEA) for nuclear material and activities and the Organization for the Prohibition of Chemical Weapons for chemical weapons and related materials and technologies. The work undertaken under resolution 59/60 must neither undermine nor overlap the function of the existing verification systems and discussions undertaken within the respective bodies.

With regard to the Convention on the Prohibition of the Development, Production and Stockpiling of Bacteriological (Biological) and Toxin Weapons and on Their Destruction, there is an ongoing process to strengthen it. The work of the panel should not undermine the ongoing process under the Convention.

With regard to missiles, since there is no international legal instrument banning their use and possession, it has thus not been identified what kind of missiles should be placed under verification.

These questions remain unanswered. They should be carefully examined before the establishment of the panel and should be duly reflected upon in the terms of the reference of the panel.

In addition, efforts should be made to operate the panel in a reasonable and cost-effective manner to ensure sound United Nations budgetary management.

We are looking forward to working towards the productive achievements of the panel to be established in 2006.

Lebanon

[Original: Arabic]
[25 April 2006 and 16 May 2006]

With reference to the above matter and note, the Ministry of Defence hereby informs you that Lebanon reiterates its support for all international initiatives and agreements aimed at disarmament and the non-proliferation of weapons that constitute a grave threat to peace and security in this region and the world, as well as its adherence to international law and the principles of the Charter of the United Nations. Lebanon also affirms that it possesses no weapons of mass destruction and that it supports the implementation of all effective deterrent measures to curb their proliferation.

With reference to the above matter and note, the Ministry draws attention to Lebanon's affirmation of the following:

- Lebanon possesses no weapons of mass destruction and is in compliance with United Nations resolutions prohibiting the use or acquisition of such weapons by terrorists;

- Lebanon provides no assistance of any kind to any group that seeks to manufacture, acquire, transport, transfer or use weapons of mass destruction;

- Lebanon has introduced laws and regulations that allow for monitoring of the export, transit and cross-border movement of weapons of all kinds, prohibit trafficking in such weapons and provide for the prosecution of terrorists, the harbouring of whom is forbidden under Lebanese law;

- Lebanon has signed ten international agreements relating to terrorism, is a member of the Financial Action Task Force on Money-laundering (FATF), which is connected with the financing of terrorism, and has created a mechanism whereby banking confidentiality may be lifted from accounts suspected of concealing financing for terrorist activities;

- Lebanon has contributed to the global efforts against terrorism but remains concerned about links between terrorism and weapons of mass destruction, especially since such weapons are at the disposal of Israeli terrorism.

Mexico

[Original: Spanish]
[16 May 2005]

Mexico maintains its position that verification of compliance with disarmament and arms control agreements is indispensable in building international confidence in the feasibility of full implementation of such agreements and hence in making the achievement of the goals of the agreements politically sustainable.

Mexico maintains its support for the 16 principles of verification adopted by the United Nations Disarmament Commission in 1988 and remains convinced that it would be useful to explore the possibility that various parts of the United Nations system could play a more active role in the implementation of certain specific verification measures and in matters related to quality control of verification systems and mechanisms, including the aspects of cost-effectiveness, efficiency and impartiality.

It will also be important to take into account the experience gained by international organizations such as the Organization for the Prohibition of Chemical Weapons and the International Atomic Energy Agency or by international verification missions, which could contribute substantially to the design of international verification measures.

Mexico reiterates that in the field of verification it is essential to strike a balance between the need for supervision, inspection, monitoring, reporting and the like and confidentiality measures and policies to protect industrial property rights. Mexico is of the view that verification systems or mechanisms based on legally binding instruments are to be preferred when defining the scope and limits of a particular verification system or mechanism.

Mexico also reaffirms that, since verification is not an end in itself, its value must be assessed in relation to what it is intended to safeguard, that is, the confidence of the international community in the credibility, transparency and physical and technological security that a particular verification system or mechanism provides.

Mexico considers it a highly valuable initiative that the General Assembly in its resolution 59/60 has requested the Secretary-General, with the assistance of a panel of government experts to be established in 2006, to explore this important topic and to transmit a report thereon, particularly in the light of the major scientific and technological advances that have been made in the field of verification.

Panama

[Original: Spanish]
[5 June 2006]

The Republic of Panama supports all multilateral efforts aimed at non-proliferation, arms limitation and disarmament, and therefore considers that the General Assembly's initiative to establish effective verification measures to ensure compliance with the relevant agreements is entirely viable and deserving of Panama's support.

Portugal

[Original: English]
[2 May 2006]

Portugal considers that adequate and reliable verification in the field of arms control, disarmament and non-proliferation activities and regimes is an essential tool to guarantee their effectiveness and is an indispensable means to build and maintain confidence among the international community.

A comprehensive set of verification measures enshrined in the treaties, conventions and regimes to which Portugal has adhered to, e.g., the Chemical Weapons Convention, the Missile Technology Control Regime, the Zängger Committee, the International Atomic Energy Agency and the Biological and Toxin Weapons Convention (though the latter is in the process of strengthening its verification procedures) already entered into force, or are about to be implemented.

In this regard, we consider that verification should be a concern of each and every country and that this concept should apply to all the appropriate non-proliferation and disarmament regimes. The issue of vital importance to the whole of the international community should be a matter of common endeavour. In this regard, we favour the initiative of setting up a panel of government experts established to explore the question of verification in all its aspects.

However, prior to establishing such a panel, it is essential to clearly define its mandate, objectives, scope and the respective financing procedures.

Moreover, we believe that the role of the United Nations in the field of verification should be retained and strengthened, through the enforcement of the relevant procedures of treaties, conventions and regimes in the field of non-proliferation and disarmament, as appropriate.

We consider that the panel of governmental experts should refrain from proposing new instruments or bodies for the purpose of verification, but rather to suggest possible ways and means to improve the effectiveness of the existing ones.

Qatar

[Original: Arabic]
[13 June 2006]

Reply of the State of Qatar

In connection with the implementation of various resolutions in the area of disarmament and international security adopted by the General Assembly, during its current (sixtieth) session, on reports of the First Committee, the Government of the State of Qatar wishes to provide the following information relating to verification in all its aspects, including the role of the United Nations in the field of verification:

- The State of Qatar has drafted legislation and laws to curb the proliferation of nuclear weapons and ensure the implementation of disarmament agreements and other agreements, in addition to which it has adopted and enforced effective measures for the establishment of domestic controls to prevent the proliferation of nuclear, chemical and biological weapons and their means of delivery;

- The State of Qatar has also created a compulsory mechanism for full implementation of all agreements concluded with international organizations.

Russian Federation

[Original: Russian]
[26 May 2005]

We believe that it would be useful to reflect on the following points in the discussion of the new draft resolution of the General Assembly on this question.

1. Events of the past few years have demonstrated that the establishment of verification regimes is a key factor in ensuring implementation of the most important agreements in the area of disarmament and non-proliferation. Work in that area must be directed towards the establishment of a reliable, effective and legally binding system for verifying observance of such international agreements.

2. An objective answer to the question of whether a State is meeting its international obligations under the international treaties it has concluded depends on the effectiveness of their verification mechanisms. That effectiveness is determined first of all by the degree to which the agreed procedures and verification techniques are improved and implemented.

3. The level of intrusiveness and the type of verification measures must depend on the nature and subject of the agreement and take into account the national security interests of each party to the agreement. Hence, such measures must be

balanced and avoid giving a unilateral advantage to any State party during the conduct of verification.

4. Under some multilateral agreements in the area of arms control, disarmament and non-proliferation, such as the Treaty on the Non-Proliferation of Nuclear Weapons and the Convention on the Prohibition of the Development, Production, Stockpiling and Use of Chemical Weapons and on Their Destruction (Chemical Weapons Convention), verification regimes and the inspection mechanisms they provide for have been established and function effectively. However, verification mechanisms have not been set up under other international treaties in this area, such as the Convention on the Prohibition of the Development, Production and Stockpiling of Bacteriological (Biological) and Toxin Weapons and on Their Destruction (Biological Weapons Convention). We believe that establishing such mechanisms will promote the increased effectiveness and viability of these international instruments.

5. One example of positive experience in the field of verification is provided by the activities of the International Atomic Energy Agency (IAEA) under the safeguards agreements and additional protocols to them. The additional protocol to the safeguards agreements is now recognized in practice as a standard for IAEA verification activities.

6. The Chemical Weapons Convention became the first global agreement subject to verification to prohibit an entire class of weapons of mass destruction. In many ways the Convention can serve as a model for implementing effective and non-discriminatory verification based on the principle of multilateralism. The verification regime it established provides for the submission of declarations on chemical facilities, continuous monitoring (routine inspections) and extraordinary measures involving a high degree of intrusiveness (challenge inspections).

7. Under the Biological Weapons Convention regime there are no agreed provisions on verification and consequently no inspection activities. That Convention's agreed mechanism for investigations through the Security Council is schematic in nature and needs further development. The absolute majority of States parties to the Biological Weapons Convention are in favour of elaborating a legally binding verification mechanism for the Convention. The Russian Federation supports such an approach.

8. With the early entry into force of the Comprehensive Nuclear-Test-Ban Treaty and its universalization, an historically unprecedented international system of treaty verification would come into being.

9. At present there is active discussion of the possibility of establishing a structure within the framework of the United Nations for verifying observance of obligations in the field of the non-proliferation of weapons of mass destruction and disarmament. That raises questions of a legal, organizational and financial nature with regard to the relationship between the new structure and existing agreements.

A more rational solution would be to improve the verification mechanisms under existing agreements and to establish new ones where necessary.

10. Further enhancement of the effectiveness of verification activities must not be financially burdensome and may be supported by additional resources, including the use of new means of monitoring.

(former) Serbia and Montenegro

[Original: English]
[31 May 2006]

Serbia and Montenegro considers that it is necessary to conduct a professional and in-depth risk analysis in the region.

There is an awareness of the long-term character of the fight against new challenges which requires a step-by-step approach. The principles and instruments of verification both at the bilateral and global levels represent an effective tool for the suppression and reduction of risks and threats.

The verification goals should not be conducive only to the reduction of the risk of the outbreak of war but also to the reduction of the scope of violence in wars. Positive and instructive examples are various aspects of verification established at the subregional level in the territory of the former Yugoslavia, where with the assistance of verification instruments soon after the end of conflicts a stable level of mutual trust among States has been established.

The United Nations commitment to consistent implementation of General Assembly resolutions 60/64 and 60/75 of 8 December 2005 may induce certain countries, faced with crises and challenges, to recognize and establish verification regimes as an instrument of prevention.

The role and influence of the United Nations in the fight against proliferation and commitment to disarmament are recognizable and indisputable.

In line with the above, Serbia and Montenegro supports General Assembly resolutions 59/60, 60/64 and 60/75.

Suriname

[Original: English]
[30 May 2006]

Suriname does not possess any weapons of mass destruction, does not plan to purchase any of those weapons in the near future and does not support countries that do possess or plan to use them.

The Surinamese Ministry of Defense promotes arms control and disarmament measures of the United Nations and shares the view that verification is essential in analysing the behaviour of countries in accordance with the provisions in these agreements. However, in the verification process the 16 principles of verification should always be taken into account and should be implemented:

- Without discrimination (verification should not apply only to third world or less developed countries but every country that is party to these agreements). It is also very important that a minimum construction be made to enable the United Nations to carry out obligations in non-signatory countries which possess, or countries that are suspected of possessing, weapons of mass destruction

- Without too much interference in internal affairs

- Without jeopardizing the economic, social and technological development of a country.

The request for inspections or information in accordance with the provisions of an arms limitation or disarmament agreement should only be used to determine if a country is acting in conformity with these agreements and should not be abused.

The Surinamese Ministry of Defense has taken note of the various proposals of the Disarmament Commissions and shares the view that:

- The establishment of a verification database within the United Nations is essential (to see the position of another State party)

- The role of the United Nations is very important, starting with research into the process, procedures and techniques of verification as well as the request to the Secretary-General to look into these matters

- On a responsive basis and with the consent of State parties to arms limitation and disarmament agreements, involvement of the United Nations in the formulation and implementation of verification provisions of specific agreements is very important.

States parties to arms limitations or disarmament agreements need to see the importance of verification in all its aspects and should give their full cooperation when they are called upon by the United Nations.

Sweden

[Original: English]
[19 May 2005]

Sweden considers the topic addressed in General Assembly resolution 59/60 to be of utmost importance. In Sweden's opinion, verification is a key element in all disarmament and non-proliferation agreements. Sweden, therefore, welcomes the establishment of a panel of experts, in accordance with paragraph 3 of resolution 59/60.

The 1980 Convention on Prohibitions or Restrictions on the Use of Certain Conventional Weapons which May be Deemed to be Excessively Injurious or to Have Indiscriminate Effects is an example of an agreement with well-developed verification provisions and an established verification mechanism. The Convention on the Prohibition of the Development, Production and Stockpiling of Bacteriological (Biological) and Toxin Weapons and on Their Destruction lacks such a mechanism. Efforts should continue to develop a verification mechanism for the Convention.

In Sweden's view, the role of the Secretary-General's roster of inspectors should be studied further, as well as possible ways and means of drawing on the capabilities within the United Nations system, including those of the United Nations Special Commission and the United Nations Monitoring, Verification and Inspection Commission, in strengthening verification efforts. The role of confidence-building measures and the potential of Security Council resolution 1540 (2004) for strengthening compliance and non-proliferation efforts also warrant study.

In this context, Sweden notes with interest that the report of the High-level Panel on Threats, Challenges and Change recommends that States Parties to the Convention on the Prohibition of the Development, Production and Stockpiling of Bacteriological (Biological) and Toxin Weapons and on Their Destruction should return to negotiations for a credible verification protocol. It also recommends that States should negotiate a new bio-security protocol to classify dangerous biological agents and establish binding international standards for the export of such agents. The Secretary-General's roster of inspectors is also highlighted.

كيفية الحصول على منشورات الأمم المتحدة

يمكن الحصول على منشورات الأمم المتحدة من المكتبات ودور التوزيع في جميع أنحاء العالم . استعلم عنها من المكتبة التي تتعامل معها أو اكتب إلى : الأمم المتحدة ، قسم البيع في نيويورك أو في جنيف .

如何购取联合国出版物

联合国出版物在全世界各地的书店和经售处均有发售。请向书店询问或写信到纽约或日内瓦的联合国销售组。

HOW TO OBTAIN UNITED NATIONS PUBLICATIONS

United Nations publications may be obtained from bookstores and distributors throughout the world. Consult your bookstore or write to: United Nations, Sales Section, New York or Geneva.

COMMENT SE PROCURER LES PUBLICATIONS DES NATIONS UNIES

Les publications des Nations Unies sont en vente dans les librairies et les agences dépositaires du monde entier. Informez-vous auprès de votre libraire ou adressez-vous à : Nations Unies, Section des ventes, New York ou Genève.

КАК ПОЛУЧИТЬ ИЗДАНИЯ ОРГАНИЗАЦИИ ОБЪЕДИНЕННЫХ НАЦИЙ

Издания Организации Объединенных Наций можно купить в книжных магазинах и агентствах во всех районах мира. Наводите справки об изданиях в вашем книжном магазине или пишите по адресу: Организация Объединенных Наций, Секция по продаже изданий, Нью-Йорк или Женева.

COMO CONSEGUIR PUBLICACIONES DE LAS NACIONES UNIDAS

Las publicaciones de las Naciones Unidas están en venta en librerías y casas distribuidoras en todas partes del mundo. Consulte a su librero o diríjase a: Naciones Unidas, Sección de Ventas, Nueva York o Ginebra.

Printed in United Nations, New York
08-30666—May 2008—3,120
ISBN 978-92-1-142262-7

United Nations publication
Sales No. E.08.IX.5